MIL

We hope you enjoy this book. Please return or renew it by the due date.

You can renew it at www.norfolk.gov.uk/libraries or by using our free library app.

Otherwise you can phone 0344 800 8020 - please have your library card and PIN ready.

You can sign up for email reminders too.

NORFOLK ITEM

30129 082 007 852

NORF
LIBRARY A

CE

Pearson Education Limited
Edinburgh Gate, Harlow,
Essex CM20 2JE, England
and Associated Companies throughout the world.

ISBN: 978-1-4058-8211-8

First published by Penguin Books 1993
Published by Addison Wesley Longman Ltd and Penguin Books Ltd 1998
New edition first published 1999
This edition first published 2008

12

Text copyright © John Escott 1993
Illustrations copyright © Bob Harvey (Pennant Illustrators) 1993
All rights reserved

The moral right of the adapter and of the illustrator has been asserted

Typeset by Graphicraft Ltd, Hong Kong
Set in 11/14pt Bembo
Printed in China
SWTC/12

Published by Pearson Education Ltd

Every effort has been made to trace the copyright holders and we apologise in advance for
any unintentional omissions. We would be pleased to insert the appropriate
acknowledgement in any subsequent edition of this publication.

For a complete list of the titles available in the Pearson English Readers series, please
visit www.pearsonenglishreaders.com. Alternatively, write to your local Pearson Education
office or to Pearson English Readers Marketing Department, Pearson Education,
Edinburgh Gate, Harlow, Essex CM20 2JE, England.

Contents

Contents

Introduction

The Chief Inspector looked around the entrance room at us. 'Mr Fox, I'll see you first, please.'

The rest of us waited. The others all seemed shocked by the theft of the necklace. We all looked at one another. Each knew what the other was thinking. Is the thief one of us?

When Paul gets a job for the summer holiday at Repsom museum, he knows it will be interesting. First there's pretty Anna Wain, the woman he's going to work with. Then there are the jewels which the museum is borrowing: the hundred thousand pound diamond necklace that belongs to the Gilbertson family.

But when someone steals the necklace, Paul's summer job gets more than interesting – it gets *frightening*. Because the police think *he* is the one who took it.

Then there's only one thing Paul can do: find the thief. And he knows where to look: it must be someone working in the museum, someone who knew what they were doing and knew the museum building well. Someone like Roger Fox, the guard, or Linda, the secretary – or even Anna Wain . . . As Paul thinks about it more and more, he begins to see who the thief is. And then he thinks of a plan, a way to prove he is right . . .

John Escott writes books for students of all ages. Most of all, he likes to write crime, detective or mystery stories. He lives in Bournemouth, a large town on the south coast of England. When he is not writing, he enjoys long walks by the sea. He also likes looking for long-forgotten books in little back-street bookshops.

Chapter 1   The Necklace

It all started when I got the job at Repsom museum. I was sixteen years old and a student. I was studying history at school, but it was the summer holiday. At first, eight weeks without having to study seemed wonderful. But I wanted to earn some money, so I got the job at the museum. It was only for six weeks.

Repsom is a large town, by the sea. It's where I live. There is a new part, with tall white buildings and modern offices. Then there is the old part of the town, with narrow streets and tiny shops. The museum is in the old part.

I was pleased to get the job because I have always been interested in history. In fact, I wanted to work at the museum when I left school.

That holiday, I was going to work with Anna Wain, a young woman about five years older than me. That was another thing that pleased me about the job!

'We'll be working in the new part of the museum, Paul,' Anna told me. 'It's not open yet. We'll be making displays, showing things that happened in Repsom in the past.'

I knew it was going to be an interesting job, and I was certain I was going to like working with Anna. I thought she was very pretty and friendly.

'We have six weeks to finish the work,' she said. 'Then the new part of the museum will be opened by a man called Patrick Yardley. He's an important businessman in Repsom. You'll meet him before the opening day because he likes to come and see how we're getting on.'

The Gilbertson necklace arrived at the museum the same day that I started work. It was a very old necklace and belonged to the

Gilbertson family. The Gilbertsons were a well-known Repsom family, although there was only one member alive now – Mrs Eve Gilbertson.

'It's belonged to my family for over a hundred years,' Mrs Gilbertson told Mr Balfour, the museum curator. 'That's almost as long as the Gilbertson family have lived in Repsom. I hope you'll look after it.'

Mrs Gilbertson was letting the museum borrow the necklace. It was going on display in the old part of the museum. Some people believed the necklace was made in France and once belonged to Marie Antoinette, the French queen. It was made of diamonds and was very beautiful.

'Is it valuable?' I asked.

'Mr Balfour said it's insured for a hundred thousand pounds,' Anna told me.

I was surprised. 'That's a lot of money,' I said.

We went to see the necklace after lunch that day. It was very beautiful and the diamonds shone brilliantly under the display lights.

It was in a locked display case with a glass front. Derek Halliday, one of the museum attendants, was looking at it through the glass.

'Hi, Derek,' said Anna. 'Keeping an eye on our most valuable display?'

He laughed. 'That's right,' he said, 'but I can't be here all the time.' He was about two years older than me and had long fair hair. He was always pushing it back off his face.

'I know the necklace is insured, but is it safe?' I said. 'What if a thief –?'

Anna was pointing at the ceiling in a corner of the room. 'See that TV camera?' she asked. 'It's filming everything that happens in this room.'

'All the rooms in the old part of the museum have TV cameras,' said Derek Halliday. 'They'll be fitted in the new part, too. There

2

It was very beautiful and the diamonds shone under the lights.

are TV screens downstairs, and a security guard watches them. Each screen shows a different room.'

'So he can see if a thief takes the necklace?' I said.

'Yes,' said Anna. 'Don't worry, Paul, nobody can steal it.'

But she was wrong.

♦

Two weeks later, Anna and I were working on a display showing the old Repsom prison and police station. We were making it look a hundred years old. There were policemen in their uniforms, and a criminal being taken into a prison cell. The cell had a real lock on the door with a big key. The policemen and the criminal were wax dummies, but they looked real.

There were more wax dummies on the displays already done. On one, there were pirates with a treasure chest full of jewels. The two wax pirates looked as if they were carrying the treasure chest up the beach. Behind them was a small boat, with another pirate sitting in it. Another display was made to look like an old shop. A wax woman was standing behind the counter.

It was my job to help build the displays. It was Anna's job to draw pictures of each one, so we knew how they were going to look. Anna also made the clothes and dressed the wax dummies, and I did most of the painting. I was enjoying the work.

The other people working in the museum were friendly. There were two museum attendants, Ian Maxton and Derek Halliday. They walked round the old part of the museum; one of them upstairs, the other downstairs. They answered questions when people wanted to know something about a display. A girl called Linda Jones worked in the museum office at the top of the building. She was only a year older than me. Then there was Cora Turner, the lady who took the money from people coming into the museum. And Roger Fox, the security guard.

That afternoon, Patrick Yardley came in to see Anna and me. He was a tall, important-looking man with a dark beard, and was dressed in a blue suit.

'Are you going to finish by the end of the month?' he wanted to know.

'We'll finish,' Anna told him. 'Paul is a good worker.'

He watched us working for a few minutes, then went into the next room and looked at the pirate display for a long time. 'I didn't know there were real pirates in Repsom,' he called out.

'There were, two hundred years ago,' replied Anna. 'They used to hide their treasure in the caves near the beach. Then a storm wrecked their ships on the rocks.'

'I didn't know that,' said Mr Yardley, coming back into the room we were working in.

He stayed and watched us for half an hour, then left.

'He looked worried,' I said.

'Some people say his business is in trouble,' said Anna. 'They say he needs money.'

'What's his business?' I asked.

'He owns jewellery shops in different towns,' said Anna. 'They're always called "Jane's jewellery" – his wife's name is Jane.'

I nodded. 'I know them,' I said, 'but I didn't know they belonged to Mr Yardley.'

We went back to work on the prison display. Anna was putting a moustache on the wax criminal. I was painting the walls of the prison.

'Don't lock me in!' I joked.

'Prison is for criminals,' she said, laughing. She pointed at the wax dummy. 'And he's the only criminal in this museum.'

Anna was wrong again.

Chapter 2   Stolen!

It was the middle of the next morning when the alarm went off. I was looking at the pictures for the display we were going to do next. It was going to show part of the old Repsom railway station.

An alarm wasn't fitted to the rooms we were working in, but I could hear it ringing downstairs.

Anna came back from the coffee machine with two cups of coffee.

'What's happening?' I asked.

'That's the security alarm,' said Anna, quickly putting down the coffee. 'Somebody must be stealing something!'

We looked at each other. 'The necklace!' we said together.

We both ran from the room, past the pirate display in the next room. Then we hurried down the stairs to the old part of the museum. I saw Roger Fox, the security guard, pushing open the door of the big room at the front of the building. The Gilbertson necklace was in that room. There was a small sign fixed to the door. The word CLOSED was written on it.

Anna and I followed Roger into the room. We looked at the display case in the centre. It was broken...and empty. *The Gilbertson diamond necklace had gone!*

Roger's face went white. He looked up at the TV camera on the ceiling. There was a newspaper covering it.

'The TV screen for this room was dark,' Roger explained. 'I knew something was wrong, so I rang the alarm and came to see.'

'Did the thief put the newspaper over the camera?' said Anna.

Roger nodded, looking worried. 'Yes. I didn't notice immediately,' he said. 'I was taking money and giving tickets to people coming into the museum.'

The display case was broken and empty. The Gilbertson diamond necklace had gone!

'Where was Cora?' asked Anna.

'She went to the Ladies room a few minutes before,' said Roger. 'I always take the ticket money when Cora isn't there. She watches the TV screens when I'm not there.'

'When did you first see the dark screen?' I asked.

'When Cora came back,' he said. 'She noticed it and said, "Look, Roger! Something's wrong!" That's when I saw it.'

'What are you going to do?' asked Anna.

'I'm going to stop people leaving the museum,' he replied. 'One of them may be the thief. Will you phone the police, Anna?'

'Of course,' said Anna, and hurried off.

Roger Fox ran off towards the main entrance.

I stared at the empty display case. If the thief was a visitor to the museum, I thought, he or she will be gone by now.

Somebody came into the room behind me and I turned round. It was Mr Yardley. 'I was just coming up to see you and Anna when I heard the alarm,' he said. 'What's happened?' Then he saw the empty display case and I didn't have to answer him.

The police arrived at 11.20 a.m. Anna and I were in the main entrance room talking to Cora Turner. Linda, the girl who worked in the office at the top of the building, was there too. She was talking to Mr Yardley.

Roger Fox unlocked the museum doors and the policemen came in. Three were wearing uniforms, two more were in ordinary clothes. One of the men in ordinary clothes told us he was Detective Chief Inspector Craven.

'Nobody has left the building since 11.10 a.m.,' Roger Fox told him. 'There were nineteen visitors in the museum when I locked the doors. They're all in the garden at the back. There's a wall around the garden and no back gate. Nobody can get out.'

'Where are all the people who work at the museum?' asked Chief Inspector Craven. He was a tall, thin man with a moustache.

8

'The two museum attendants are in the garden with the visitors,' said Roger Fox. 'Mr Balfour, the curator, has been out all morning. The rest of us are here, in this room.'

Chief Inspector Craven nodded to the other man in ordinary clothes. He and one of the policemen wearing uniforms went out to the garden. The Chief Inspector looked around the entrance room at the rest of us.

'I'll begin with some questions,' he said.

Chapter 3   Questions

'Can I use that room?' the Chief Inspector asked Roger Fox. He pointed to the door of Mr Balfour's office, which was in the corner of the entrance room.

'Yes, I'm sure that will be all right,' said Roger. 'Mr Balfour will not be back for half an hour.'

Chief Inspector Craven and one of the policemen in uniform went across to Mr Balfour's room. 'Please wait until I ask you to come in,' the Chief Inspector told us. 'Mr Fox, I'll see you first, please.'

Roger followed them into Mr Balfour's room while the rest of us waited. I looked at the others. They all seemed shocked by the theft of the necklace.

'This is terrible,' said Mr Yardley. 'Has anybody told Mrs Gilbertson?'

Cora Turner shook her head. 'Not yet,' she said. 'Perhaps we should wait for Mr Balfour to come back.'

'Yes, I think you're right,' said Mr Yardley. He looked at Anna. 'I came back to see how you were getting on with the new displays. I was on my way up the stairs when I heard the alarm.'

'Mrs Gilbertson is going to be very unhappy,' said Linda, sitting on the edge of the ticket desk.

'The thief has got away,' said Cora Turner. 'I noticed the dark TV screen at eleven o'clock, but several people left the building after that. Roger closed the museum doors at ten minutes past eleven. That gave the thief ten whole minutes to get away.'

The security television screens were behind the ticket desk. All the screens were showing rooms in the museum now, I noticed.

They all seemed shocked by the theft of the necklace.
'This is terrible,' said Mr Yardley. 'Has anybody told Mrs
Gilbertson?'

We all looked at one another. Each knew what the other was thinking. *Is the thief one of us?*

Roger came out of Mr Balfour's room. 'The Chief Inspector wants to see you next, Cora,' he said.

Cora looked nervous when she went in to see Chief Inspector Craven. Then we heard the museum doorbell ring and the other policeman in uniform opened the door. Two police-women came in.

I knew one of them, but she didn't seem to recognize me. I was glad. There was something I didn't want her to remember.

'They're here to search everybody,' said Roger. 'The Chief Inspector told me.'

'Search!' said Linda.

Roger nodded. 'He wants to be certain we don't have the necklace on us,' he said.

'They're not searching me!' said Linda.

'Then the police will think you're hiding something, Linda,' said Roger. 'They'll think you're the thief.'

'But how can I be the thief?' she said, angrily. 'I was at the top of the building in the main office, with Derek Halliday.' She suddenly looked embarrassed and her face became red. 'He – he was asking me to go to the cinema with him on Saturday night.'

Roger smiled. 'I hope you enjoy the film,' he said. 'But how do you know it was exactly eleven o'clock when he was in the office?'

'Because Derek asked me how long it would be before Mr Balfour came back to the museum,' said Linda. 'I looked at the office clock and saw it was eleven o'clock. Then I told Derek that Mr Balfour was coming back in another hour.'

'Then you and Derek have nothing to worry about,' said Roger. 'You were both together when the theft happened.'

Linda looked unhappy, but I knew she was going to allow a policewoman to search her. She doesn't want the police to think she's a thief, I thought.

Cora came out of Mr Balfour's room and told Anna to go in next. Anna smiled at me when she went past. 'We don't have to worry, Paul,' she said. 'We were together when the necklace was stolen, weren't we?'

I watched her go into the little office. Anna went to the coffee machine and came back just before the security alarm went off, I thought. How do I know she didn't steal the necklace before she came back with the coffee? But I didn't want to believe that. I liked Anna.

I went to see Chief Inspector Craven when Anna came out. He was sitting at Mr Balfour's desk, and the policeman in uniform was standing behind him. Both the Chief Inspector and the other policeman were tall men, and they seemed to fill the little room.

'Miss Wain tells me you were with her all morning,' said the Chief Inspector.

'Yes, that's right,' I replied. She hasn't told him about fetching the coffee, I thought.

He looked at me for several moments before speaking again. Then he said, 'How long have you worked at the museum?'

'Two weeks,' I said.

He looked at his book of notes. 'Two weeks and one day,' he said, 'according to Miss Wain.'

'Yes,' I agreed with him.

'In fact, you started work the same day that the Gilbertson necklace arrived,' he said.

'Yes, I suppose I did,' I said.

'Don't you *know*?' he shouted.

I was becoming nervous. 'Yes, all right, I started the day the necklace arrived,' I said.

'And now it's gone,' he said quietly.

He made it seem as if the two things went together – I started work here, then the necklace was stolen.

'I didn't take it,' I told him.

He looked at me thoughtfully. 'There have been lots of valuable things on display in this museum,' he said, 'and they have always been safe. Then you come to work at the museum and a valuable necklace is taken. Strange, don't you think?'

'I'm not a thief!' I said.

The office door opened and the other detective came into the room. Chief Inspector Craven looked up at him.

'Yes, Todd?' he said.

'I've questioned the visitors and the museum attendants,' said the other man. 'They all say they didn't go into the room where the necklace was on display. The "closed" sign was on the door.'

'But the door wasn't locked, according to the security guard,' said the Chief Inspector. 'It would be easy enough to go in.'

'All the visitors have said they'll be searched,' said Todd. 'If they have the necklace, we'll find it.'

'Not if they were able to hide it somewhere in the museum,' said Chief Inspector Craven. 'Search the other rooms they were able to get into.'

'OK,' said the other man. He didn't look pleased. 'But I'm sure the thief got away before the museum doors were locked.'

The Chief Inspector looked annoyed. 'Just do it, Inspector.'

Inspector Todd went out of the little office and Chief Inspector

'. . . you started work at the museum the same day that the
Gilbertson necklace arrived,' he said.

Craven looked back at me. 'You can go,' he said. 'You will be searched in a few minutes. Tell the office girl I want to see her next.'

I went back into the entrance room and saw Mr Balfour coming in the museum door. He was a short man with not much hair. He looked around at everybody, then saw the policemen and policewomen. His eyes opened wide with surprise.

'What's happening?' he said. 'Is something wrong?'

♦

Everybody was searched, but the necklace wasn't found. Mrs Gilbertson was informed about the theft, and Mr Balfour told us she was very angry.

'She has the necklace insured,' said Mr Balfour, 'but that doesn't make it any better. It was stolen when it was here in our museum. That makes me very unhappy.'

The visitors were allowed to go home and we all went back to work. The museum didn't open again until two o'clock because the police wanted to search it.

They looked in all the rooms that were open for visitors. Then Inspector Todd came to the new part of the museum.

'Nobody usually comes in here except for us,' Anna told him.

'And Mr Yardley,' I reminded her.

'But he only comes when we're here,' said Anna.

'You ran downstairs when you heard the alarm, didn't you?' asked Inspector Todd. He looked very tired.

'Yes, we did,' Anna said. 'We can just hear it up here.'

'Then the thief *could* have come up here after you went downstairs, I suppose,' he said.

'Yes, I suppose he could,' said Anna.

'He . . . or she,' said the Inspector.

He began to look at the new displays, not moving any of the wax dummies. It was obvious he didn't want to do it, he was too tired.

16

*He began to look at the new displays, not moving any of the
wax dummies. It was obvious he didn't want to do it.*

'I've been working all night,' he told us. 'There was a robbery at a post office in the centre of town last night.'

'Paul's just painted some of the displays,' Anna warned him. 'The paint is still wet.'

After that, he didn't look very closely. He was afraid of getting paint on his suit.

'This is a waste of time,' he said after some minutes. 'I'm certain the thief escaped with the necklace before the museum doors were locked. There was plenty of time, wasn't there?'

We agreed that there was, and after ten more minutes he stopped looking.

It was a big mistake.

Chapter 4   The Hiding-Place

The next day, I noticed that part of the wall at the back of the pirate display was still not quite finished.

'I thought you finished that a week ago,' said Anna. She looked annoyed.

'So did I,' I said. 'I didn't notice that bit of wall. Sorry.'

'Don't worry about it,' she said. 'Nobody can see it easily. It's more important to finish the other displays.'

I didn't want to make her even more annoyed, so I didn't return to the pirate display. Instead, I worked on the old Repsom railway station display.

'Have the police found the thief yet?' I asked Anna.

'No,' she said, shaking her head. 'They're hoping he'll try to sell the necklace in Repsom, and then they may catch him.'

'Or her,' I said, more to myself than to Anna.

She looked surprised. 'Yes, or her,' she said.

'The police suspect me, you know,' I told her.

'I know,' she said. 'They asked me lots of questions about you yesterday. I told them you were with me all morning. I said it wasn't possible for you to steal the necklace.'

'But I wasn't,' I said.

'Pardon?' said Anna.

'I wasn't with you *all* morning,' I said. 'There was the time when you went to get the coffee. It was about the same time the theft happened.'

She didn't look at me, and she didn't speak for a moment. Then she said, 'I don't believe you're the thief, Paul. I like you and I'm certain you're honest. And I'm sure you don't think I'm the thief. Do you?'

But not all the jewels were false . . . One necklace was very valuable indeed. It was the Gilbertson diamond necklace!

'No,' I said. It was true, I didn't believe Anna was a thief.

She left the museum before me that afternoon. 'I have to go to the dentist,' she told me. 'See you in the morning, Paul.'

It was after Anna left that I decided to finish painting the wall at the back of the pirate display. It didn't look right. Somebody might notice it later and I'll be blamed, I thought. It won't take long to do.

I got a paintbrush and a tin of paint, then climbed on to the display. I had to move one of the wax pirates and the wooden treasure chest to reach the wall.

It took me just five minutes to do the painting. Afterwards, I lifted the wax pirate back on to the display. Next, I picked up the treasure chest. I was putting it back when I suddenly noticed something. The jewels in the chest were arranged differently.

I remembered putting the false jewels into the treasure chest a week before. I knew the way they were arranged because I did it. But now they looked different.

Somebody's moved them! I thought.

I immediately began to look through the chest. It was just a wooden box, painted to look like a treasure chest. It was as false as the jewels.

But not all the jewels *were* false, I discovered when I took them out.

One necklace was very valuable indeed.

It was the Gilbertson diamond necklace!

21

Chapter 5   A Mystery to Solve

I must tell Roger Fox! was my first thought. We must call the police and I'll tell them where the necklace was hidden. Mrs Gilbertson will be pleased, and everyone at the museum will be happy.

I was moving towards the door when I stopped.

Wait a minute, I thought. What am I doing? The police already suspect me of stealing the necklace. If I tell them I've found it, will they believe me? Or will they say I stole it, but then got frightened and *pretended* to find it? Will they still think I stole Mrs Gilbertson's necklace?

I remembered the way Chief Inspector Craven looked at me when we were in Mr Balfour's office. It was as if he didn't *want* to believe me.

What can I do? I thought. Then I began to think about the real thief. Why did he or she hide the necklace in the treasure chest? Because it's a good hiding-place. Nobody would specially notice the necklace together with all the false jewellery. And it was underneath all the other jewellery, not very easy to see until you moved things.

Suddenly, I heard somebody coming up the stairs. I was still holding the necklace in my hand and quickly pushed it back into the treasure chest. Then I covered it with the other jewels and put the wooden box back on the display.

Moments later, Roger Fox walked into the room.

'Hallo, Paul,' he said. 'Are you still working?'

'I'm going home now,' I told him. 'I just wanted to finish painting that bit of the wall.'

I was glad there was no security camera in that room. Nobody saw me discover the necklace and its hiding-place, I thought. But the thief also knew there was no camera. He or she knew they could hide the necklace up here without being seen.

I went downstairs with Roger. The museum was closed now, but Mrs Morgan was talking to Derek Halliday in the main entrance room. She was the cleaner and came in every evening at this time. Mrs Morgan and my mother were old friends and she knew me from when I was a small boy.

'Hallo, Mrs Morgan,' I said.

'Hallo, Paul,' she answered. 'How are you?'

'I'm very well,' I said.

'Are you enjoying your job here?' she asked.

'Yes, I am,' I said.

I left the museum and began walking home. There were a lot of tourists in the town because it was summer. I went down on to the beach and walked along near the sea. People were still swimming, although it was early evening. Small boats with white sails moved across the water.

The sun was warm on my face as I walked. It was a good feeling, but I needed to think. I was worried. What was I going to do next?

Then I had another thought. What was the *thief* going to do next? Obviously he or she wasn't going to leave the necklace in the treasure chest for very long. And it would be much harder to discover who the thief was when the necklace was gone.

What actually happened? I thought. When did the thief hide the necklace in the treasure chest? Was it immediately after he or she stole it? Before the alarm went off? It could have happened that way. I was working in the other room, cutting a piece of wood with an electric saw. That saw makes a lot of noise and it's difficult to hear anything in the next room. Anna was getting the coffee. Unless . . .

Perhaps it was Anna who hid the necklace, I thought, but I didn't want to believe it. But then I remembered another thing.

It was Anna who stopped Inspector Todd looking carefully at the displays, I thought. She told him some of the paint was wet, and he didn't check them very well after that. Did Anna do that on purpose? It was also Anna who told me not to paint the wall behind the pirate display, earlier today. Did she do that because she didn't want me to find the necklace?

I was confused. Why would Anna steal a necklace? Did she need money?

Another person needed money, I remembered. Mr Yardley needed money, according to Anna. The man's business wasn't doing very well. What was Mr Yardley doing when the theft happened? He *said* he was coming up to see Anna. But was that true or was he telling lies?

Nobody saw him coming up the stairs, I thought. Perhaps he went into the room where the necklace was on display, then put the newspaper over the camera and stole the necklace.

I remembered the name of the newspaper over the camera. It was the *Daily Chronicle*. Mr Yardley always carried *The Times* when he came to see Anna and me.

But perhaps he bought an extra newspaper yesterday, I thought. And he would know where to sell the necklace. Jewellery was his business. I preferred to think Mr Yardley was the thief, rather than Anna.

I was almost certain about one thing. The thief was somebody who knew about the pirate's treasure chest before the theft. He or she knew there was somewhere to hide the necklace, so that nobody would find it quickly. That meant it was somebody who knew the pirate display was finished.

Mr Yardley knew, I thought. But so did everyone who works in the museum. But they all had alibis . . . didn't they?

I decided I was going to find out. But I would have to be quick. The thief might come back for the necklace at any time.

Chapter 6   Suspects

That evening, I went to a cinema in the centre of town. It was a good film but I was having trouble keeping my mind on the story. I kept on thinking about the stolen necklace. Was the thief collecting it from its hiding place in the museum now? Would it be gone tomorrow?

After the film was over, I went down to the beach again for some fresh air. The sea was silver under the moon, the water moving gently up and down the beach. There were a few other people walking – young couples with arms around one another, and a woman running with her dog.

There was a café near the beach and I went in for a cup of coffee. There were only a few people inside.

A couple at a table in the corner seemed to be arguing about something. Suddenly, I realized the woman was Cora Turner. The man with Cora looked a bit like her. I remembered somebody saying Cora had a brother.

I couldn't hear their conversation but I could see Cora was angry. The man looked worried and afraid. Then Cora's voice got louder and I heard something she said. Something which made me listen more carefully.

'. . . you'll have to tell them to wait,' she was saying. 'I can't get the money any faster. You were a fool, Greg. Anyone who gambles is a fool.'

I didn't hear any more. Soon after, Cora and the man left the café. She didn't see me, and I was glad. I've always found other people's arguments embarrassing.

But I remembered her words. Why does Cora have to get money in a hurry? I thought. Is it because her brother gambles

I couldn't hear their conversation but I could see Cora was angry.

and loses money? I remembered the face of the man and knew she was getting the money for him. He was afraid of something. Or somebody. Did he borrow money from someone to gamble?

How will Cora get money? I thought. By selling the Gilbertson necklace? Is *she* the thief?

I began to think about her alibi. It was Cora who saw the dark TV screen when she came back from the Ladies room, according to Roger Fox. She told him and he rang the alarm before running upstairs. But perhaps she put the newspaper over the camera and stole the necklace when she was supposed to be in the Ladies room. She knew Roger was busy selling tickets to people coming into the museum, and that he wouldn't be watching the TV screens at the same time.

Perhaps that's how Cora did it, I thought. Or am I wrong?

◆

On my way to the museum the next day, I saw Ian Maxton, one of the museum attendants. I was walking along the narrow street leading to the museum, between lines of little shops. Shopkeepers were opening their shop doors or brushing the steps outside as I went past.

Ian was coming out of a shop with a newspaper. He saw me walking towards him.

'Hallo, Paul,' he said.

'Hi, Ian. Where's your motor bike?' I asked him. 'You usually ride it to work, don't you?'

'I – I had a bit of an accident last week,' he said. 'It's at the garage, for repairs.'

'Were you hurt?' I said.

He shook his head. 'No, I was OK,' he said. 'The motor bike was damaged and so was the car.'

'Car?' I said.

'I was coming round a corner and went into the back of a car,' Ian said. He looked worried. 'I was to blame because I was going too fast. There was quite a lot of damage.'

I liked Ian and was sorry to hear about his accident. He asked me how Anna and I were getting on with the new displays. I told him we hoped to finish them by the end of the month.

'I like the pirate display,' he said. 'I was looking at it the other day.'

We were going into the main entrance room of the museum when he dropped his newspaper. I picked it up and gave it to him. It was the *Daily Chronicle*.

'Thanks,' he said, hurrying off to get ready for work.

♦

I was about to go upstairs when Mr Balfour arrived. He rushed through the entrance doors, a worried look on his round face.

'Ah, Paul,' he said. 'I wanted to talk to you. Come into my office, will you?'

I followed the curator into the little room and he sat down behind his desk. He pointed to another chair and I sat down as well.

'Anna tells me you are doing some good work on the new displays,' said Mr Balfour. 'I'm glad.'

I smiled and tried not to look too pleased with myself. 'I like Anna,' I said. 'We work well together.'

'I gave you the job because you seemed to be the right person for it,' he said. 'Also, Mrs Morgan knows you and says you're an honest young man.'

'I'm honest, yes,' I agreed with him. 'Perhaps there have been times when I've been in trouble, but I'm honest.'

He looked thoughtful for a moment, then said, 'The police were asking a lot of questions about you. They were worried because the

28

Gilbertson necklace was stolen only two weeks after you came here. They also know it's the first thing to be stolen from the museum. They think it's odd.'

I could feel my face getting hot with anger. 'I didn't steal it, Mr Balfour,' I said as calmly as I could.

He looked at me carefully. 'No, I don't think you did, Paul,' he said. 'I just thought you should know they suspect you.'

'I already knew,' I told him.

'I went to see Mrs Gilbertson again last night,' he said. 'She's still very unhappy. The police have told her they hope to catch the thief, but she doesn't believe they will. Her family has always been important in Repsom, and Mrs Gilbertson is very proud of that. She has lived alone since her husband died eight years ago. I think she's a lonely woman, with only her family history to think about. She seems worried that people will forget how important the Gilbertson family have been. She decided to lend the necklace to the museum to remind people, I think.'

'I'm sorry her necklace was stolen,' I said, 'but I didn't steal it.'

'The theft has been a shock to us all,' said Mr Balfour. 'When I came back that morning, I could hardly believe the things Roger Fox told me. It was a pity I wasn't here when it happened. If Cora isn't at the ticket desk, I sometimes help Roger by watching the screens.'

Did the thief know that? I thought. Did he or she know there was nobody watching the screens, because Mr Balfour was out?

'Who knew you were out that morning?' I asked after a moment.

He was surprised by the question. 'Cora and Roger knew,' he said. 'They were at the ticket desk, talking to Derek Halliday. "See you at about twelve o'clock," I told them as I left. Linda knew as well, because she had some of my letters to type. I told her to have them finished by twelve o'clock.'

At that moment, Mr Balfour's phone rang and I left him to answer it.

Cora, Roger, Derek Halliday and Linda. One of them must have told Anna, because she also knew Mr Balfour was out. In fact, nearly everybody knew he was out.

It wasn't much help.

Chapter 7   Time for an Alibi

I hurried upstairs, hoping Anna was not there yet. I wanted to check that the necklace was still in the treasure chest. But Anna was working on the railway station display, putting a railwayman's uniform on one of the wax dummies.

'Good morning, Paul,' she said.

'Hi, Anna,' I said.

'I see you painted that bit of wall on the pirate display,' she said.

I felt embarrassed. 'I did it after I finished work, last night,' I said. 'I just thought it would look better.'

She smiled. 'You were right, Paul,' she said. 'Sorry I was in a bad mood yesterday. It was probably because I was going to the dentist in the afternoon.'

I smiled back at her. 'That's OK,' I said. I was always ready to forgive Anna almost anything.

We worked on the railway display for two hours. I was building the ticket office. It looked very real when Anna put the wax railwayman in it.

'It's time for coffee,' she said. 'I'll get it.'

I waited until she was gone, then hurried into the other room. The pirate display looked the same. The treasure chest seemed to be in the same place. Nothing seemed to be different. I lifted out the false jewels that were on the top of the chest . . . and there was the Gilbertson necklace underneath.

The thief didn't come back for it last night, I thought. How much longer before he or she does?

I quickly covered the necklace with the other jewels and went back into the next room. A few minutes later, Anna arrived back with two cups of coffee.

'I walked to work with Ian Maxton this morning,' I told her. 'He was telling me about his motor bike accident.'

Anna drank some of her coffee. 'Did Ian tell you his motor bike wasn't insured for an accident?' she asked.

'No, he didn't!' I said, surprised.

'Well, it wasn't,' she said. 'That means he has to pay for the damage to his bike, *and* the damage to the car. It's going to cost about two thousand pounds.'

I was shocked. 'Does Ian have two thousand pounds?' I asked.

'I'm sure he hasn't,' replied Anna.

'Where will he get the money?' I said.

'I don't know,' she said.

So he's another person who needs money, I thought. It was then I remembered Ian bought the *Daily Chronicle* newspaper.

The morning passed quickly and it was soon time for lunch.

'I have some shopping to do,' Anna said. 'I shan't be coming to the café today.'

There was a small café opposite the museum and some of the people working at the museum went there each day. I crossed over the road and went inside. It was busy and there were no empty tables. Derek Halliday was eating at a table near the window and I went across.

'Can I sit with you?' I asked him.

'Of course,' he said.

I sat down and looked at the menu, trying to think about food. But something was worrying me. What was it? I couldn't remember. Something Mr Balfour said that morning? I didn't know, but seeing Derek Halliday reminded me there was *something*.

A waitress came over and I ordered a cheese salad.

'What display are you working on now?' asked Derek. He was eating fruit and ice-cream.

'The old Repsom railway station,' I said. 'We'll finish it this

There was a small café opposite the museum . . . Derek
Halliday was eating at a table near the window.

week. There aren't many more displays to do after that. Two or three more weeks' work.'

'You'll want another job then,' he said.

'No, I have to go back to school,' I said.

'Good idea,' he said. 'Jobs are hard to find at the moment.'

'How long have you worked at the museum?' I asked.

'A year,' he replied.

'What did you do before?' I asked.

'I was a gardener,' he said.

I suddenly knew the thing that was worrying me, and it *was* something Mr Balfour told me.

'Linda and you were in the office when the necklace was stolen, weren't you?' I said.

Derek nodded. 'That's right,' he said.

'Linda said you asked her when Mr Balfour was coming back,' I said.

'Did she?' he said. 'I can't remember asking that, but perhaps I did.'

'It's strange if you did,' I said.

'Why?' he asked.

'Because you already knew,' I answered. 'You were talking to Cora and Roger when Mr Balfour left that morning. He told them he was coming back at twelve o'clock. Didn't you hear him?'

Derek finished eating his ice-cream. 'Yes, I did,' he said after a moment. 'Linda's mistaken, I didn't ask that question.'

'Was she wrong about the time, too?' I said. 'She said she knows you were both in the office at eleven o'clock, because she looked at the clock.'

'She's right about the time,' said Derek. 'I remember looking at my watch.'

'Did you hear the alarm ringing?' I asked.

'No, we didn't hear that,' he said. 'It only rings downstairs in the museum. The office is at the top of the building, as you know.'

'When did you find out about the theft?' I said.

'When I went downstairs again, a few minutes later,' he said. 'I heard the alarm then.'

The waitress arrived with my cheese salad.

'Do you want a cup of coffee?' she asked Derek.

'No, thanks,' he said. 'I have to make a phone call before I go back to work. See you later, Paul.'

I began to eat, watching Derek through the café window as he went across the road to a public telephone, outside the bank.

Why did Linda say Derek asked that question if he didn't? I thought. Was she telling a lie? Derek knew when Mr Balfour was coming back and didn't need to ask.

But it didn't seem to matter. They were both together when the theft happened. They both had an alibi.

Unless they're both telling lies! I thought suddenly.

Chapter 8   Trouble for Me

Inspector Todd was at the museum when I got back from lunch. He was in the main entrance room, talking to Mr Balfour, when I came in.

Have they found the necklace on the pirate display? I thought, feeling worried. Do they think I put it there?

'Come into my office please, Paul,' said Mr Balfour. He looked very serious.

'What's wrong?' I asked when we were in the little room. Inspector Todd was looking at me but he said nothing.

'You haven't been completely honest with me, Paul,' said Mr Balfour.

I didn't understand. 'What makes you think that?' I said.

'Why didn't you tell me you were in trouble with the police before you came here?' he said.

I began to feel cold inside. I knew the time he meant. 'But – but that was two years ago,' I said. 'I was only fourteen, and I wasn't to blame. There were two older boys and –'

'I know you weren't guilty of the crime,' said Mr Balfour, interrupting. 'Inspector Todd has told me that. He's told me it was the other boys who stole the things from the shop. You were just foolish enough to be with them when it happened.'

'But perhaps there were other times when you stole things,' said Inspector Todd. 'Times when you've not been caught.'

'No!' I shouted. 'That's not true!'

'Now you're working here,' the Inspector went on. 'What happens two weeks after you start? Something is stolen. Strange, isn't it?'

'I didn't steal the necklace,' I said. 'You must believe me.'

'It was one of the policewomen who recognized you,' said Inspector Todd. 'She didn't remember who you were at first, but today she did.'

'I remembered her,' I said. 'She came to the shop when the things were taken.' I looked at Mr Balfour. 'It was three packets of cigarettes,' I told him. 'They stole three packets of cigarettes, and the shopkeeper saw them. I didn't steal anything, I was just with them. I didn't even know they were going to do it.'

Inspector Todd walked across to the door of the little office. 'I just want you to know we haven't forgotten it,' he told me, smiling. It wasn't a nice smile. 'We'll be keeping a careful eye on you in the future.'

He went out and closed the door behind him. I waited for Mr Balfour to say something. The curator looked tired and unhappy.

'I like you, Paul,' he said, sadly. 'I want you to know that. I'm certain you didn't steal the Gilbertson necklace, but the police do suspect you. That makes things difficult for me. I think it would be better if you found another holiday job after this week.'

I didn't speak for several moments. My head was full of angry thoughts but I didn't know how to say them. I understood Mr Balfour's problem. If Mrs Gilbertson discovered the police suspected me, she would blame Mr Balfour for allowing me to work here. People said Mrs Gilbertson was not a nice person. They said she got angry with people and was often in a bad mood. But Mrs Gilbertson was an important person in the town. She could make trouble for the museum.

'I'll leave at the end of the week,' I said quietly.

◆

37

I told Anna.

'It's not fair!' she said. 'You haven't done anything wrong.'

'The police think I have,' I said. 'They think I stole the Gilbertson necklace, and I've been in trouble with them before.' I explained about the theft in the shop when I was fourteen.

'You were only a child then!' she said. 'Lots of children get into trouble. They don't all become criminals later on.'

'I know,' I replied.

'If only they could find the necklace and the real thief,' said Anna. 'Then everything would be all right and you could stay at the museum.'

'Yes,' I said.

But I know there was another problem. A much bigger problem.

If the police *do* find the necklace before the thief moves it, I thought, they'll find my fingerprints on it. I've touched it twice since it was stolen. Why didn't I wipe them off?

It was a bad mistake. Why didn't I think of it before? Now it might be too late. The thief might be coming to get the necklace out of its hiding-place that night. What could I do? When could I get the necklace and wipe my fingerprints off it?

If the thief is coming to the museum tonight, I thought, then I ought to be here to catch him!

It was dangerous, but it was something I had to do. The police believed I was the thief and I was going to have to leave my job at the museum. I had to do *something*, and catching the thief was the best thing I could think of doing.

I thought about the various suspects – people who needed money, like Cora and Ian Maxton and Mr Yardley.

But how could I be sure the real thief would come to the

museum? Was there a way to *make* the thief collect the stolen necklace that night? Was there a way to trap him?

I began to think.

Half an hour later, I had an idea. I wasn't sure if it would work, but I knew I had to try it.

Chapter 9   The Strange Policeman

At five o'clock that afternoon, I told Anna we had a problem on the pirate display.

'What sort of problem?' she asked, surprised.

'Come and see,' I said.

We went into the next room and I took her round to the back of the display. Each display was built on a wooden platform, a metre off the ground. The platforms were held up by thick pieces of wood. The pieces of wood were fixed underneath the platform.

I got down on my hands and knees and pointed under the platform. 'Look,' I said.

Anna got down beside me. 'What am I supposed to be looking at?' she said.

'Over there,' I said, pointing.

She looked at the two thick pieces of wood under the centre of the platform. Each of them seemed to have fallen down.

'How did that happen?' said Anna. 'I don't understand it.'

'I don't know,' I said, trying not to look at her. 'But they can't stay like that. I'll have to stand them up and fix them again.'

'That will be dangerous, Paul,' said Anna. 'You'll have to get underneath the platform. What happens if it comes down on you? The display on this platform is heavy. You could be badly hurt.'

'I can move the display off the platform,' I said. 'It will take time, but it's the only thing to do to be really safe.'

'You're right,' Anna agreed with me. 'When will you do it?'

'Tomorrow morning,' I said. 'There isn't enough time this afternoon. We finish work in half an hour.'

During the next thirty minutes, I told everyone about the pirate

I got down on my hands and knees and pointed under the platform. 'Look,' I said.

display. Everyone except Mr Balfour. I didn't want to see him again that day. But I told all the others in the museum – Roger Fox, Cora Turner, Linda Jones, Derek Halliday and Ian Maxton. I wanted them all to know I was going to move everything off the platform.

I even telephoned Mr Yardley at his Repsom shop. He was surprised to get a call from me.

'I know you're interested in the displays,' I said. 'I thought I'd tell you we've got a bit of a problem with one of them.'

'Which display is that?' he asked.

'The pirate display,' I told him.

'What's wrong with it?' he said, after a moment.

I explained about the pieces of wood under the platform. 'It's a pity I have to waste all tomorrow morning doing it,' I told him, 'but we can't leave it. It's not safe.'

I was glad nobody was near the pirate display earlier that afternoon, to see me go under it. Nobody to see me cut through the pieces of wood with a saw, then *push* them over.

Of course, it was a dangerous thing to have done. I was afraid the platform might come down on top of me at any moment. But it was an important part of my plan to trap the thief, and I had to do it.

◆

I left work at the usual time, making sure several people saw me. But I didn't go home. Instead, I phoned my mother and told her I was staying at a friend's house that night. Then I went into a café and had a pizza and some salad.

At 6.30 p.m. I went back to the museum. It was closed and there were no cars in the car-park outside. But I knew somebody was working inside.

I rang the doorbell.

It was some minutes before the door opened. Mrs Morgan was standing there.

'Hallo, Paul,' she said, looking surprised. 'Sorry to keep you waiting, but I was cleaning the office at the top of the building.'

'I forgot my library book when I left earlier,' I said as she let me into the museum. 'It has to go back to the library today. I'll just go and fetch it, then I'll be going again.'

She didn't seem to know I was leaving my job at the museum. What would she say when she found out?

Perhaps she won't need to find out, I thought. Perhaps by tomorrow the thief will be caught.

'What time is it?' she asked.

I looked at my watch. 'Just after 6.30,' I said.

She nodded. 'I thought it was,' she said. 'The office clock seems to be all right now.'

'What do you mean?' I said.

'It was ten minutes fast the other day,' she said. 'I noticed it when I was cleaning the office.'

'Ten minutes fast?' I said. 'What day was that?'

'Monday,' said Mrs Morgan. 'But I put it back to the right time the same evening.'

'The day the necklace was stolen,' I said.

'Pardon?' she said. 'Yes, that's right. The day Mrs Gilbertson's necklace was stolen. A terrible thing to happen, wasn't it?'

'Yes,' I said, but I was thinking about the office clock. How strange that it was fast on *that* day, I thought.

'Will you make sure the museum door is locked when you leave, Paul?' said Mrs Morgan, going on up the stairs to the office.

'Yes, OK,' I said.

I needed somewhere to hide. A place where I could see the pirate

*It took me two minutes to get the uniform off the wax dummy,
and another minute to put it on me.*

display, but wouldn't be seen. If the thief came to collect the necklace, I wanted to see that person's face.

But first I had something to do.

I climbed on to the platform and walked carefully over to the treasure chest. Then I took out the Gilbertson necklace and wiped it with my handkerchief. I didn't want the police to find any of my fingerprints on it, if the thief didn't come. Then I put the necklace back in the treasure chest.

Next, I looked round for a hiding-place. The old Repsom prison and police station display was in the next room. I could see it through the open door. I looked at the prison cell with the big key in the lock. But it wasn't a good place to hide. Anyone could see through the cell door.

Then I looked at the wax dummies. Two policemen, and a criminal being taken into the cell. Suddenly, I had an idea. It seemed a crazy idea, but . . .

One of the wax policemen was about my size. His uniform would fit me, I thought.

It took me two minutes to get the uniform off the wax dummy, and another minute to put it on me. I laughed as I put on the policeman's hat. I make a good policeman! I thought. Then I put my clothes and the wax dummy behind the display.

An hour later, Mrs Morgan finished her work in the office and came downstairs. I stood completely still on the prison display, like a real wax dummy. But she didn't come into the rooms where Anna and I worked. A few minutes later, I heard her switch on the burglar alarm, then go out of the museum door downstairs, and lock it behind her.

I didn't know how long I would have to wait for somebody to arrive.

But now I was sure I knew the thief's name.

Chapter 10   A Thief Is Caught

I seemed to be standing there for hours. I didn't dare put on a light. The moon was shining through the window and I looked at my watch. I could just see that it was midnight.

How much longer? I thought.

And then I heard a noise.

It was the sound of glass breaking and it came from the back of the building. Then I heard the back door being pushed open. As this happened, the burglar alarm began to ring . . . but only for a few moments, then it stopped again.

The thief doesn't have a key, I thought. But I knew that already. Only Roger Fox, Mr Balfour and Mrs Morgan had keys for the museum door, and I knew the thief wasn't one of them. But the thief *does* know the place to switch off the burglar alarm. And this made me even more certain I knew who the thief was.

Somebody was coming up the stairs.

I stood very still on the prison display. I tried to breathe quietly, but I could hear the sound of my heart.

The person was carrying a torch and the light suddenly came into the next room. It moved round, passing over the displays. Then it shone into the room I was in. The light was bright in my face but I kept my eyes still and it passed over me. The thief thought I was just another wax dummy.

All I could see behind the torchlight was the shadow of a person. I couldn't see the face in the dark.

The torchlight was shining on the treasure chest now. The person was moving towards it. A hand lifted the false jewellery out of the chest, then took out the Gilbertson necklace. The diamonds shone brilliantly in the torchlight.

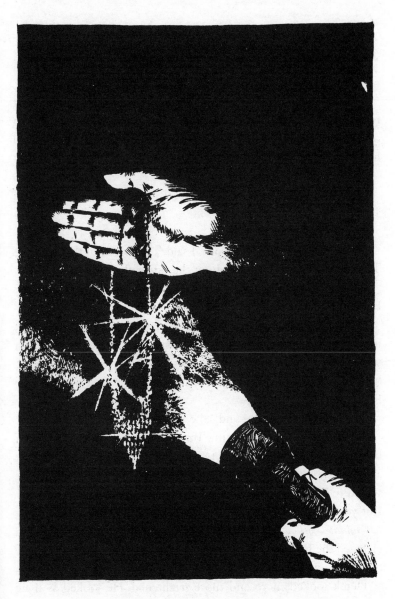

A hand took the Gilbertson necklace out of the chest. The diamonds shone brilliantly in the torchlight.

I heard the thief give a little laugh.

I knew that laugh.

'Hallo, Derek,' I said.

Then I moved quickly and switched on the light in the next room. It was suddenly as bright as day. Derek Halliday was standing on the pirate display, looking frightened and amazed. He was still holding the necklace.

'What –?' he began.

'Are you surprised to see me, Derek?' I said. 'Yes, I'm sure you are.'

'How. . . ?' he said.

'How did I know it was you?' I said. 'I didn't, until this evening. Then Mrs Morgan told me about the office clock.'

He looked as if he was suddenly feeling ill. 'What do you mean? I – I don't understand.'

'Before she told me about the clock, there was something I didn't understand,' I said. ' "Why did Derek ask Linda when Mr Balfour was coming back?" I kept asking myself. "He already knew. Derek heard Mr Balfour say when he would be back, when he was with Roger and Cora." '

'I didn't ask Linda!' he said. 'She was telling lies!'

I pretended not to hear him. 'But when I heard about the clock being fast, I knew the answer,' I went on. 'You *wanted* Linda to look at the time and see it was eleven o'clock. Then, afterwards, she would tell everyone you were together when the theft happened. But you weren't together, were you, Derek? Because it was really *ten minutes before eleven* when Linda looked at the clock. You changed the time on it before she arrived that morning. You made the clock ten minutes fast.'

Derek looked more and more frightened. He looked as if he might run, but he knew he wouldn't get far. At last he let out a long breath and said, 'I – I was going to put the clock right again the next morning, before Linda arrived at the museum. But Mrs Morgan noticed it before I had a chance.'

'There's still something I don't understand,' I said. 'What were you going to do with the necklace? Sell it? Who was going to buy it? Do you know people who buy stolen jewellery?'

Derek shook his head. 'No,' he said.

'Why did you steal it then?' I asked.

He didn't speak for a minute. He was trying to decide the best thing to do. Then he said, 'Somebody paid me to steal it.'

Now it was me who was surprised. 'Who?' I asked.

He opened his mouth to speak again . . .

There was a loud *bang*! from near the door. It was the sound of a gun! I turned to see who was shooting, and a dark shape ran across the room, covered in a long coat with a hood. The hood covered the person's face.

I watched the hooded person grab the diamond necklace from Derek's hand. Derek was on the floor now, blood pouring from his shoulder. The person in the hood lifted the gun again. *The gun was pointing at Derek* . . .

I moved quickly and switched off the light.

'Put on that light!' somebody screamed. I heard somebody running towards the door. I ran into the next room and heard the person following me. It was dark, except for the moon.

I ran behind the prison display and got down on the floor, hoping the hooded person wouldn't see me. I could hear him or her moving around in the dark. But it was somebody who didn't know where things were in the room. Several times, he or she knocked against wax dummies.

Then I heard feet coming up on to the platform of the prison display. 'Where are you? I know you're in here,' the voice said. It was a woman's voice.

I could just see her moving. She was holding out a hand,

The sound of the gun filled the whole room with its terrible noise. I was extremely frightened.

feeling the way. Without realizing it, *she was walking into the prison cell.*

I waited until she was inside the cell, then I jumped up from my hiding-place. I ran across, shut the cell door, and quickly locked it.

The hooded shape turned round. I saw the gun in a white hand. *It was pointing at me.* I pulled the key out of the lock on the cell door, then jumped away.

The sound of the gun filled the whole room with its terrible noise. I was extremely frightened. But moments later, I was running down the stairs.

The nearest phone was in Mr Balfour's room. I switched on every light I passed, then ran into the little office. The phone was on the desk.

I grabbed it with a shaking hand.

Chapter 11   The Final Surprise

The police cars and the ambulance arrived together. I heard their alarms screaming through the streets, and I opened the museum doors ready to let them in.

Inspector Todd was one of the first to reach the door.

'Where are they?' he wanted to know.

'Upstairs,' I said. 'Be careful. One of them has a gun.'

'You told us that over the phone,' he said. 'We've come prepared.'

And I saw several policemen were carrying guns.

But the hooded person caused no trouble.

'Don't shoot me!' she screamed from the locked cell. 'You can have my gun!'

We heard her throw the gun across the floor. One of the uniformed policemen ran inside and picked it up. Then Inspector Todd switched on the lights.

Derek Halliday was still on the pirate display in the next room. We could see him through the open door. His eyes were closed and his face was the colour of dirty snow. The ambulance men ran across to him.

The woman in the hooded coat was still inside the cell, but now we could see the face under the hood. And I knew who she was.

'Mrs Gilbertson!' I said.

♦

It was the afternoon of the next day and I was sitting in Mr Balfour's room. The curator was sitting behind his desk. Detective Chief Inspector Craven and Inspector Todd were in two more chairs.

The curator was sitting behind his desk. Detective Chief Inspector Craven and Inspector Todd were in two more chairs. I finished telling them my story.

I finished telling them my story.

'You were lucky she didn't kill you,' said the Chief Inspector.

'I had to try and trap the thief,' I told him. 'You all thought I stole the necklace.'

He looked uncomfortable. 'We were wrong, Paul,' he said. 'I'm sorry.'

'But I still don't understand,' I said. 'Why did Mrs Gilbertson pay Derek Halliday to steal her necklace?'

'She needed money,' said Inspector Todd. 'Everyone thinks she's rich, but she isn't. She's told us she has hardly any money left.'

'The necklace was insured for one hundred thousand pounds,' said the Chief Inspector. 'Mrs Gilbertson was planning to get the insurance money *and* sell the necklace, later on.'

'Derek Halliday used to work for her before he came to the museum,' said Inspector Todd. 'He was her gardener. One day, she discovered him stealing some money from her desk in the house. So she knew he wasn't honest and that he might be able to help her.'

'It was Mrs Gilbertson who asked me to give Derek Halliday a job,' said Mr Balfour. 'About a year ago.'

'She's been planning this for a year?' I said, surprised.

The Chief Inspector nodded. 'Probably longer,' he said. 'Halliday's job was to steal the necklace and hide it somewhere in the museum. She knew the police were probably going to search the people who worked here. He had to leave the necklace in its hiding-place for a week, then take it to her.'

'But yesterday he heard you were going to move everything on the pirate display,' Inspector Todd told me. 'He knew he would have to get the necklace before it was found. He phoned Mrs Gilbertson and told her he was going to get the necklace at midnight.'

'He also told her he wanted more money for stealing it, or he would go to the police,' said Chief Inspector Craven. 'It was then that Eve Gilbertson knew Halliday would always be asking her for more and more money to keep quiet. She had to do something – so she decided to kill him.'

'She followed him to the museum,' said Inspector Todd. 'She watched him break the glass on the back door. She saw him open the door and go inside. Then she followed him up the stairs. You know what happened after that.'

'Yes, I do,' I said. 'It's something I'll never forget.'

Derek Halliday didn't die, but he did go to prison.

Mrs Gilbertson also went to prison, for a very long time.

And me? I finished working at the museum at the end of that month, then I went back to school.

'Come back and see me when you've finished school, Paul,' Mr Balfour told me. 'There'll be a job here for you, if you want it.'

'I'll be back,' I said, smiling.

And I shall.

ACTIVITIES

Chapters 1–2

Before you read

1 Look at the Word List at the back of the book. What are the words in your language?

2 Which word(s) on the Word List:
   a are people?
   b looks like a person, but isn't real?
   c is a room in a prison?
   d is a piece of jewellery?
   e is a box full of valuable things?
   f is something you do for your car? (Then, if you have an accident, you don't have to pay.)

3 Read the Introduction at the beginning of the book, then answer these questions.
   a Where does Paul get a summer job?
   b What belongs to the Gilbertson family?
   c Will the story be funny, exciting or sad?

While you read

4 Write answers to these questions.
   a What is the Gilbertson necklace locked in? ....
   b What are the two wax pirates carrying? ....
   c Who watches the TV screens? ....
   d Who owns jewellery shops in different towns? ....
   e What is covering the TV camera on the ceiling? ....
   f Who takes the ticket money when Cora isn't there? ....
   g How many visitors are in the museum? ....

56

After you read

5 Who says or thinks these words?
   a 'We'll be making displays, showing things that happened in Repsom in the past.'
   b 'It's belonged to my family for over a hundred years.'
   c 'I know the necklace is insured, but is it safe?'
   d 'All the rooms in the old part of the museum have TV cameras.'
   e 'Some people say his business is in trouble.'
   f 'The TV screen for this room was dark.'
   g 'I was just coming up to see you and Anna when I heard the alarm.'

6 Work with another student. Have this conversation.
   Student A: You are Anna. You are phoning the police. Tell them what has happened at the museum.
   Student B: You are the policeman who takes the phone call. Ask questions about the necklace and about Mrs Gilbertson. Who do you need to tell about the theft? Who will go to the museum? You have to decide and tell Anna.

Chapters 3–4

Before you read

7 In these chapters, do you think:
   a Anna will find the necklace?
   b Paul will find the necklace?
   c Chief Inspector Craven will find the thief?
   d Linda will run away from the museum?
   e Anna will fall in love with Chief Inspector Craven?
   f someone will bring back the necklace?
   g none of these things will happen?

8 Answers these questions.

   a Who does the Chief Inspector question first? ....

   b What time did Cora Turner notice the dark
TV screen? ....

   c Who was with Linda when the office clock
said eleven o'clock? ....

   d Who went to the coffee machine and came
back just before the alarm went off? ....

   e Who is too tired to move any of the wax
dummies? ....

   f The wall behind one of the displays needs
more paint. Which display is it? ....

   g Where does Paul find the diamond necklace? ....

After you read

9 Choose the correct words to complete the sentences about the
story.

   a Paul started working at the museum ... the necklace arrived.

     • before • when • after

   b ... stolen before Paul worked at the museum.

     • Nothing was • Two things were • A lot was

   c Inspector Todd is tired and thinks the thief ... the necklace.

     • hid • dropped • left with

   d Anna says she ... Paul.

     • suspects • half suspects • does not suspect

10 Work with another student. Have a conversation.

   Student A: You are Mr Balfour, the curator of the museum. You
have to telephone Mrs Gilbertson to tell her about the
theft of the necklace. What are you going to say?

   Student B: You are Mrs Gilbertson. You are very angry about the
theft. What are you going to say?

Chapters 5–6

Before you read

11 In these chapters, do you think:

    a Paul tells Chief Inspector Craven that he's found the necklace?

    b The necklace disappears again?

    c Paul runs away with the necklace?

    d Paul leaves the necklace in the treasure chest to catch the thief?

    e Mr Balfour catches the thief?

    f none of these things happen?

While you read

12 Are the sentences right (✓) or wrong (✗)?

    a The police suspect Paul of stealing the necklace.   .....

    b Roger Fox sees Paul put the necklace back in the
treasure chest.   .....

    c Mr Yardley's business isn't doing very well.   .....

    d Mr Yardley always carries the *Daily Chronicle* when
he comes to the museum.   .....

    e Cora's brother, Greg, is a gambler.   .....

    f Ian Maxton rides a motor bike, but he had an accident
last week.   .....

    g Ian Maxton drops his newspaper. It's *The Times*.   .....

    h Mr Balfour sometimes watches the TV screens.   .....

After you read

13 Put these events from the story into the correct order.

    a Paul hears somebody coming up the stairs.

    b Paul walks along the beach.

    c Paul sees Cora and her brother in the café.

    d Roger sees Mrs Morgan talking to David Halliday.

    e Paul puts the necklace back in the treasure chest.

14 Work with another student. Have this conversation.

> *Student A:* You are Cora's brother, Greg. You need money quickly. You've borrowed money from some dangerous people. Now you have to pay them back but you can't. You want Cora to help you.

> *Student B:* You are Cora. You are angry about Greg's gambling, but you're frightened for him. You can get money by selling some of your things, but it takes time. What advice can you give him?

Chapters 7–8

Before you read

15 In these chapters, do you think:
   a Anna finds the necklace in the treasure chest?
   b Mr Balfour finds the necklace in the treasure chest?
   c Mr Balfour discovers that Paul once did something bad?
   d Paul leaves the museum job and goes back to school?
   e Anna leaves the museum and get another job?
   f none of these things happen?

While you read

16 Answer these questions.
   a What display is Anna working on? ....
   b How much money does Ian need to pay for the damage to his bike and the car? ....
   c Who does Paul sit with at the café? ....
   d How long has Derek Halliday worked at the museum? ....
   e What did the two older boys steal from the shop? ....
   f What has Paul forgotten to wipe off the necklace? ....

After you read

17 Who says these words?

    a 'I see you painted that bit of wall on the pirate display.'

    b 'What display are you working on now?'

    c 'No, I have to go back to school.'

    d 'Linda's mistaken. I didn't ask that question.'

    e 'You haven't been completely honest with me, Paul.'

    f 'We'll be keeping a careful eye on you in the future.'

    g 'It's not fair. You haven't done anything wrong.'

18 Work with another student. Have this conversation.

    Student A: You are the policewoman who comes to the shop after the cigarettes are taken. You question Paul about the theft. You don't believe his story.

    Student B: You are Paul when he was younger. You try to make the policewoman believe you didn't steal anything. It was the two older boys.

Chapters 9–11

Before you read

19 Which of these people do you suspect the most? Why?

    a Anna Wain

    b Ian Maxton

    c Derek Halliday

    d Roger Fox

    e Cora Turner

    f Linda Jones

While you read

20 Answer these questions.

    a What is each display built on? ....

    b Who is working in the museum after 6.30 p.m.? ....

    c How many police dummies are there? ....

d Who changed the time on the office clock
on the day of the theft?

....

e Where does Paul lock the person with the
gun?

....

f Who worked for Mrs Gilbertson before he
came to the museum?

....

After you read

21 Correct the mistakes in these sentences.

  a Paul damages the platform under the prison display.

  b Anna tells the other people in the museum that he is going to move the display the next day.

  c He knows the thief will come in the morning.

  d Derek was with Linda at 10.50 and at 11 o'clock on the day of the theft.

  e Mr Balfour paid Derek to steal the necklace.

  f Derek told Mrs Gilbertson he would go to the police if she didn't give him more money, so she killed him.

  g She planned get the insurance money and keep the necklace.

22 Paul suspects different people at different times in the story. What are his reasons for suspecting each of these people?

  a Anna Wain

  b Mr Yardley

  c Cora Turner

  d Ian Maxton

  e Derek Halliday and Linda Jones

23 Work with another student. Have this conversation.

  Student A: You are Mrs Gilbertson. You need Derek Halliday's help to steal the necklace. Tell him about your plan.

  Student B: You are Derek Halliday. You want to get some money, but you're not sure about Mrs Gilbertson's plan. It's dangerous. You want more money than she offers.

Writing

24 You are Paul. You are studying history at school. Write a letter asking for a job at the museum for the summer holidays.

25 You are Anna. Write a letter to a friend. Tell him or her about your work on the new displays. Tell him or her about Paul, your young assistant.

26 You are Paul. Write your diary for the day when the necklace is stolen.

27 Write a news report about the opening of the new part of the museum. Tell your readers about the new displays. Make it sound as interesting as you can.

28 Choose a picture in the book and write about it. What can you see in the picture? Who can you see? What are they doing?

29 Look back at the first part of Chapter 11 (page 52) Tell this part of the story again through the eyes of Inspector Todd instead of Paul.

30 Have you ever had a holiday job? Write about it. What did you do? Did you enjoy it? Is it something you want to do again?

31 Write about the book for a newspaper. Is it a good story? Why (not)?

32 Because Paul is telling the story, nobody describes him. But we know quite a lot about him from some of the pictures in the book. We also know what he's interested in, and something about the things he did in the past. Write about him. Say what he looks like and what sort of person he is.

33 Write another story about the theft of something valuable – a book, a painting, a horse, some treasure? It can be a true story or something imaginary.

WORD LIST

alarm (n) an electric bell that rings when somebody enters a room or touches something

alibi (n) something that proves you were somewhere else at the time of a crime

cave (n) a large natural hole under the ground or in the side of a hill

cell (n) a small room where a prisoner is kept

curator (n) a person who is in charge of a museum

display (n) an arrangement of things for people to look at

dummy (n) a model of a person that is used instead of a real person

gamble (v) to play games in which you win or lose money

go off (v) to suddenly make a loud noise (bombs and alarms)

grab (v) to take hold of something in a sudden violent way

hardly (adv) almost not

hood (n) a part of a coat or jacket that covers your head; someone whose head is covered in this way is **hooded**

insure (v) to pay money to an **insurance** company so that you will receive money if something bad happens

motor bike (n) a two-wheeled vehicle with an engine

museum (n) a building where you can see interesting old things, usually connected with art, science or history

necklace (n) a piece of jewellery that is worn around the neck

nod (v) to move your head up and down as a way of saying 'yes'

obvious (adj) clear and easy to notice or understand

pirate (n) someone attacks ships to steal things from them

saw (n) a tool used for cutting wood by moving it backwards and forwards

screen (n) the part of a TV or computer that shows pictures

security (n) keeping things or people safe from crime

suspect (v/n) to think that someone may be guilty of a crime; a person who you think may be guilty is a **suspect**

theft (n) the crime of a thief

torch (n) a small electric lamp that you carry in your hand

treasure (n) a collection of things like gold and jewels; a big box of *treasure* is a **treasure chest**

valuable (adj) having a high value in money

wax (n) a hard form of oil used for making models of people

wipe (v) to use a cloth to clean dirt from something

wreck (v) to damage a ship so badly that it sinks

Better learning
comes from fun.

Pearson English **Readers**

There are plenty of Pearson English Readers to choose from
- world classics, film and television adaptations, short stories, thrillers,
modern-day crime and adventure, biographies, American classics,
non-fiction, plays ... and more to come.

For a complete list of all Pearson English Readers titles, please contact
your local Pearson Education office or visit the website.

pearsonenglishreaders.com